# GRASSLANDS
## UNDER THREAT

PAUL MASON

Raintree

**www.raintreepublishers.co.uk**
Visit our website to find out more information about Raintree books.

**To order:**
☎ Phone 0845 6044371
🖹 Fax +44 (0) 1865 312263
📠 Email myorders@capstonepub.co.uk

Customers from outside the UK please telephone +44 1865 312262

©Raintree is an imprint of Capstone Global Library Limited, a company incorporated in England and Wales having its registered office at 7 Pilgrim Street, London, EC4V 6LB - Registered company number: 6695582

"Raintree" is a registered trademark of Pearson Education Limited, under licence to Capstone Global Library Limited

Text © Capstone Global Library Limited 2009
First published in hardback in 2009
Paperback edition first published in 2010

Edited by Louise Galpine and Rachel Howells
Designed by Richard Parker and Manhattan Design
Picture research by Hannah Taylor and Rebecca Sodergren
Production by Alison Parsons
Originated by Dot Gradations Ltd.
Printed in China by Leo Paper Products Ltd.

ISBN 978 0 431020 60 0 (hardback)
13 12 11 10 09
10 9 8 7 6 5 4 3 2 1

ISBN 978 0 431020 67 9 (paperback)
14 13 12 11 10
10 9 8 7 6 5 4 3 2 1

**British Library Cataloguing in Publication Data**
Mason, Paul
Grasslands under threat. – (World in peril)
577.4'8

A full catalogue record for this book is available from the British Library.

**Acknowledgements**

We would like to thank the following for permission to reproduce photographs: Alamy p. **11** (Wesley Hitt); Corbis pp. **6** (Kazuyoshi Nomachi), **13** (Arthur Morris), **18** (Liba Taylor), **24**; eyevine p. **23** (Polaris/ Adriana Zehbrauskas); FLPA p. **22** (Nigel Cattlin); Getty Images pp. **4** (Roy Toft), **8** (Minden Pictures/ Tim Fitzharris), **21** (Andrea Booher), **25** (Brandi Simons); Imagestate p. **15** (Design Pics); Panos p. **16** (Caroline Penn), **17** and **19** (Dieter Telemans); Photolibrary pp. **7** (Craig Aurness), **9** (Glow Images), **10** (Frank Krahmer), **12** (Stockbyte), **20** (Christian Heinrich), **26** (Fresh Food Images/ Joff Lee), **27** (Animals Animals/ M Harvey/ ABPL); Reuters p. **14** (Radu Sigheti).

Cover photograph of park rangers and volunteers trying to put out savannah fires in the Nairobi National Park, reproduced with permission of Panos (Fred Hoogervorst).

We would like to thank Michael Mastrandrea for his invaluable help in the preparation of this book.

Every effort has been made to contact copyright holders of material reproduced in this book. Any omissions will be rectified in subsequent printings if notice is given to the publishers.

All the Internet addresses (URLs) given in this book were valid at the time of going to press. However, due to the dynamic nature of the Internet, some addresses may have changed, or sites may have changed or ceased to exist since publication. While the author and Publishers regret any inconvenience this may cause readers, no responsibility for any such changes can be accepted by either the author or the Publishers.

# Contents

Some words are printed in bold, **like this**. You can find out what they mean by looking in the glossary.

# Where do grasslands grow?

There are grasslands on every **continent** except Antarctica. Grassland of some kind covers at least a third of the land on Earth. In nearly a quarter of the world's countries, grassland makes up at least half of the land.

Grasslands grow in all sorts of temperatures, from hot to cold. In dry climates, the grasses grow short. This kind of grassland is often called **steppe**. Where there is more water, the grasses grow taller. This kind of grassland is often called **prairie**. A third type of grassland has a mixture of grasses with scattered plants and trees. This is called **savannah**.

Grasslands are an important part of our **environment**. They are home to many different plants and animals, especially birds and insects. Grasslands absorb rainfall, feeding it into rivers and underground stores called **aquifers**. Much of our food is grown on farms in grassland areas.

Today, the world's population is growing. Our increasing demands for food and water mean that many of the world's grasslands have disappeared – and the rest are under threat.

What would it be like to spend your days looking after sheep, instead of going to school? **Nomads**, such as these in Tibet, have always roamed across grasslands. They hunt for food, and their animals **graze** on the grass.

Nomads were the first people to live on grasslands. But then farmers realized that some plants could be grown for food. Crops had to be planted near water, so most early farms were near rivers.

This giant cornfield is in Iowa, USA. In North and South America, most grassland is now farmland. Many of the grassland plants, animals, and people have lost their homes.

In Africa and Asia, only about a fifth of grassland is used to grow crops. But as the world's population gets bigger, so does our demand for food. Many of these grasslands are also under threat from farming.

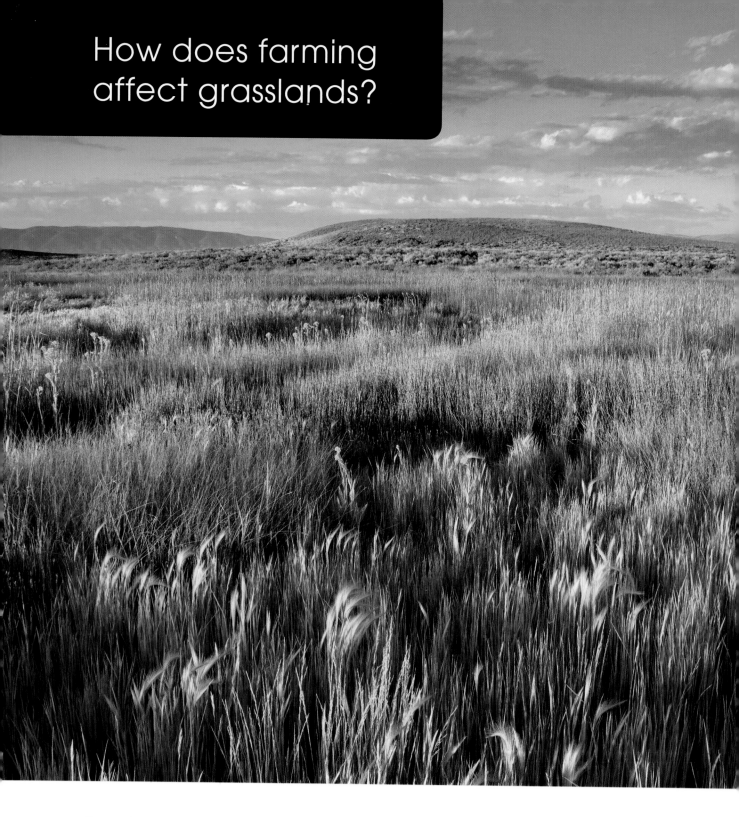

# How does farming affect grasslands?

Imagine exploring this grassland in the Arapaho Wildlife Refuge in Colorado, USA. It is home to many different plants and animals.

Natural grasslands are full of **genetic diversity**. This is when living things from the same **species** have slightly different characteristics. Genetic diversity helps protect against diseases. If a disease affects one kind of sagebrush, for example, it does not necessarily affect every kind. A few sagebrush bushes survive.

How many types of plant grow on this farmland? When crops are planted, a single type of plant replaces the variety that was once there. Many insects, birds, and other animals lived off the plants that no longer grow there. These creatures find it difficult to survive.

If only one crop is planted, and a disease attacks the crop, many plants will be killed. Before, very few plants would have died.

# What happens when the insects disappear?

Insects, such as this bee, **pollinate** plants, helping them to **reproduce**. Insects go from plant to plant, drinking the nectar. Pollen from one plant is carried to the next. Once there, pollen helps the plant to make seeds.

Insects are also food for birds and animals. Bigger, **predatory** birds and animals then eat these smaller ones. Insects are one of the first links in the grassland **food chain**.

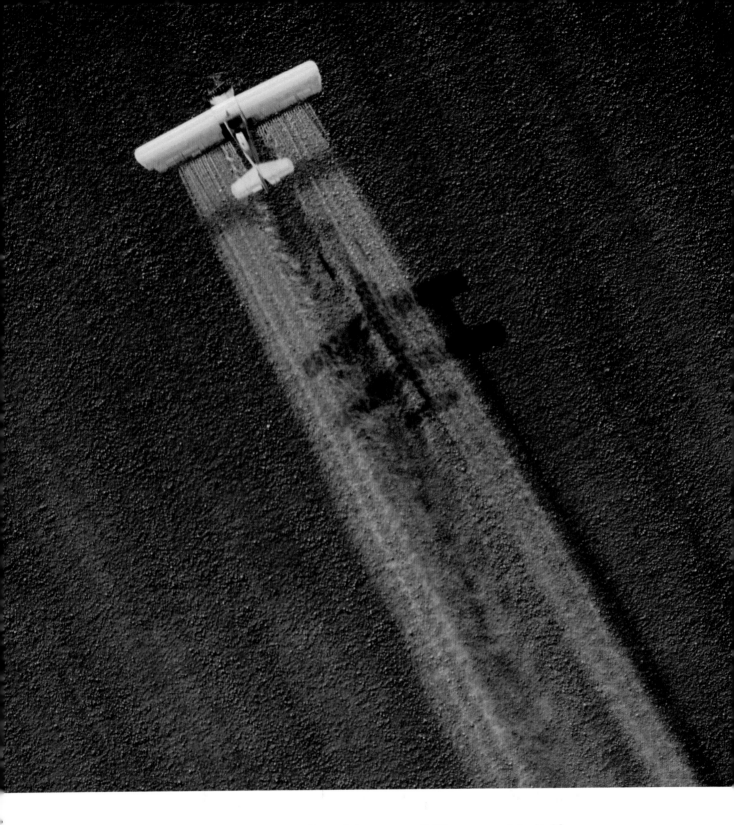

Would you want to stand under this spray? You wouldn't if you knew what was in it! To stop insects eating crops, farmers use planes like this one to spray **pesticides** on their land. These chemicals kill the "**pests**" – but they also kill other insects.

When the insects die out, it means there is no food for the birds and other animals that eat the insects. These bigger animals also start to disappear from the area.

# How do changes to grasslands affect birds?

Grasslands are important to many different birds. Many birds live all year in grassland regions, feeding off the plants and insects.

Grasslands are also important to **migratory** birds. These birds spend winter in one place and summer in another. As they travel between the two places, the birds stop off in grasslands to eat, gathering strength before travelling on. Many also breed in grassland areas.

Now that many grassland areas are used for growing food, the plants and insects that birds used to eat have disappeared. The number of local birds has fallen.

Migratory birds, too, find it hard to get enough food during their stopovers. Unless they build up their strength, the birds may not finish their journey. They may also fail to **reproduce** successfully. As a result, the number of migratory birds steadily falls.

# What is happening to grassland animals?

This giant herd of wildebeest is walking through grasslands in Africa. In the past, grasslands were home to many different animals. They ranged from tiny insects to giant herds of huge creatures such as buffalo and wildebeest. There were also **predators** such as lions, hyenas, coyotes, and snakes. This variety of living things is called **biodiversity**. Today, the biodiversity of grasslands is under threat as never before.

Once roads are built across grasslands, animals start to suffer. Many are killed trying to cross. Roads, fences, and pipelines break the grassland into smaller parcels of land. **Migration** routes are blocked. Animals find it harder to find a mate, because they have a smaller area in which to look for one. Many grassland animals have also lost their natural **habitat** because grasslands have been turned into farms. In the end, biodiversity decreases.

# What is at the bottom of the well?

These people are collecting water from a pump. Grassland communities have always used wells to get at underground water stores. These underground water stores, called **aquifers**, come from rain soaking through the grassland soil. When the water reaches hard, waterproof rock, it stops soaking down. Instead, it builds up into a water store. Some aquifers are hundreds of kilometres across, and take hundreds of years to fill.

Would you enjoy transporting all your water from a well by camel each day? Such jobs are becoming more common as grassland wells dry up. The reason is that today, cities and farmers are drawing huge amounts of water from grassland aquifers.

So much water is being taken that aquifers are being drained much faster than they can be filled by rainfall. The level of water in the aquifers has fallen so low that wells can no longer reach it.

These herdsmen from India are **grazing** their cattle on grasslands near their village. Cattle and other animals have been grazed on grasslands such as these for thousands of years.

In the past, grazing animals had little impact on the grasslands. The herders moved from place to place. They only came back to an old pasture when the grasses and plants had had a chance to grow again.

Why do you think this herd of cattle is stirring up such a dust storm? Today, there are many more animals grazing on the land. They quickly strip all the grass from the soil, which is left bare.

With so many cattle around, the grasses never get a chance to grow back. Without grass roots to hold it in place, the soil is blown away. The land becomes a **desert**. This process is known as **desertification**.

# Who should grasslands benefit?

This lion has caught a springbok, a type of antelope. The **carcass** will feed other lions, before smaller animals, such as vultures, start to peck at it. As the dead animal starts to rot, it will provide food for insects and other tiny creatures.

A male lion needs about 260 sq km (100 sq miles) of grassland territory to survive. If this territory was converted into farmland, it could provide food for many people.

Can you imagine what it would be like to stand in a queue, waiting for your daily food ration? Already, many of the world's people go hungry each day. By 2050, there may be three billion more people in the world than in 2000. They will all need to be fed.

Is it right that grasslands should be kept as they are so that animals can continue to live undisturbed, when the land could be used to feed people?

# What is the difference between these two crops?

Can you see a difference between these two crops? The one above is maize being grown in Alsace, France. In amongst these maize plants are some that have **resistance** to **pests** and diseases that would kill other maize plants. If pests or diseases strike, some of the plants will survive. This resistance variety among plants is important, as it stops whole varieties of plant being wiped out.

This crop looks like the one in France, but it is not. These plants are in Mexico, which is where many of the world's varieties of maize come from. In 1998, a farmer accidentally planted genetically modified (GM) seeds in Mexico.

The GM plants have started to spread, mixing with other varieties. If this continues, all the plants may end up the same. The plants would lose their ability to survive some pests and diseases.

# Could we make better use of our farmland?

These corn fields are in Iowa, USA. Today, the biggest threat to grasslands is being turned into farmland for growing grain. Over 70 per cent of the United States' tallgrass **prairie** grasslands, for example, have now been turned into farmland.

Corn is one of the world's most important foods. Some of the world's corn is ground into flour. The flour is used to make bread, cakes, biscuits, and other foods.

Would this grain be better used to feed humans? More than half of the world's grain is used to feed farm animals, which are later killed and sold as meat.

It takes five times as much grain to feed a person on a meat-based diet as it does on a grain-based diet. If the grain was eaten by people instead of fed to animals, the patch of grassland the grain was grown on would feed five times as many people.

# Is there hope for grasslands?

Vegetarian meals like this one place less strain on grasslands than meat. Deciding not to eat meat as often is one way of helping grasslands, and the **environment** in general.

In dry areas, people can also help the grasslands by using less water. This means the **aquifers** will not be drained, and there will be enough water below the grassland surface.

Have you ever dreamt of going on a safari like this one in Kenya?
If you did, it might help the grasslands survive. But how?

Safari tourism brings foreign visitors and money to poor countries.
This makes them keen to keep the grasslands in their natural state.
As a result, governments have turned some areas into national
parks to stop farmers moving into the area.

# WHAT DID YOU FIND OUT ABOUT GRASSLANDS?

**Why are grasslands important?**
Tip: think about the **habitats** that grasslands provide to plants, animals, and insects, and the things that humans use grasslands for. Page 5 gives a good summary, but also read over the chapters throughout the book for specific examples.

**How many types of grassland are there?**
Hint: look through the book at the different types. Grasslands can be sorted depending on whether the grass is tall or short, whether it grows thickly or thinly, or whether there are a few trees and bushes there as well.

**What are the differences between grasslands and farmlands?**
Tip: look at pages 6–7, 8–9, and 10–11 to try and come up with an answer. Making a list of the features of grasslands and farmlands will help you to see their differences clearly.

**Why are the grasslands shrinking?**
Hint: there are lots of reasons why the amount of grassland has been getting smaller and smaller. But the main reason is mentioned on page 5, and appears in photographs on pages 7, 9, 11, 18, and 25.

**How do humans affect the grasslands?**
Tip: look at the photographs on pages 11, 15, 17, 19, and 23 for some clues.

**What would be the effect of saving grasslands?**
Hint: using what you've learned from this book, try making two lists, of the good and bad things about leaving grasslands as they are today.

**What will happen to humans if the grasslands disappear completely?**
Tip: don't forget, the effects could be felt far from the grasslands themselves.

**What will happen to birds, animals, and plants if the grasslands disappear?**
Hint: would disappearing grasslands only affect the wildlife that live in the grasslands themselves? Or would it also affect other living things?

**Could we feed more people using the same farmland as today?**
Tip: pages 24–25 will give you some ideas about this. The answer may not be a simple yes or no: it might be that it could be done, but people are not willing to give up the things they would need to give up. What do you think?

**What are some things you can do to help save the grasslands?**
Hint: one topic you might think about is food. What you eat, how it is grown, how it is transported, and where it comes from might all be things that have an effect – even though your dinner table is nowhere near a grassland!

# Glossary

**aquifer** underground store of water

**biodiversity** range of different living things in an environment. An area's biodiversity includes its animals, plants, fungi, and tiny creatures such as bacteria.

**carcass** dead body

**continent** large land mass. There are seven continents: Europe, North America, South America, Africa, Asia, Australasia, and Antarctica.

**desert** area of land where there is low rainfall and very dry conditions, making it difficult for most plants and animals to survive

**desertification** when land turns into a desert

**environment** landscape, soil, weather, plants, and animals that together make one place different from another

**food chain** group of plants and animals that are linked together because each one further up the chain depends on the ones below it for food

**genetic diversity** when living things from the same species have slightly different characteristics. One groundhog might be better able to survive a disease than another, because its body naturally produces resistance to the disease.

**graze** when an animal feeds on fresh food, such as grass, that grows on the land

**habitat** local environment that is home to particular types of plants and animals

**migration** spending different parts of the year (usually winter and summer) in different places

**nomad** person who moves from place to place with their animals

**pest** damaging creature. To a farmer, anything that damages or eats crops is a pest.

**pesticide** chemical that is used by farmers to stop insects, and plants such as fungi, destroying their crops

**pollinate** to move pollen from one plant to another. Pollination helps plants to reproduce (make new plants).

**prairie** grassland where tall grasses grow

**predator** animal that hunts other animals for food

**reproduce** make offspring or young. When dogs have puppies they are reproducing.

**resistance** immunity to something

**savannah** grassland where grasses are mixed with shrubs and a few trees

**species** particular type of creature. For example, lions, leopards, and cheetahs are three different species of cat.

**steppe** grassland where the conditions do not allow the grass to grow as high as on a prairie

# Find out more

## Books

*Earth in Danger: Habitat Destruction*, Helen Orme (Bearport Publishing, 2008)

*Grasslands*, Michael Allaby (Facts on File, 2006)

*World Cultures: Living in the African Savannah*, Nicola Barber (Raintree, 2008)

## DVD

*America's Lost Landscape: The Tallgrass Prairie* (2005)

Tallgrass **prairies** were once a key feature of the American landscape, home to unique people, plants, and animals. This documentary tells the story of how, between 1830 and 1900, almost all the tallgrass prairies were turned into farmland. This happened in just a single lifetime.

## Websites

**www.panda.org/news_facts/education/middle_school/habitats/grasslands**

This webpage is part of WWF's website and it explains all about grasslands.

**www.worldbiomes.com/biomes_map.htm**

By clicking on the key of this map you can see more about the different **habitats** (biomes) of the world, including grasslands.

# Index